DAYBREAKS

Daily Reflections for
LENT and EASTER

PAULA D'ARCY

PAM HUMMELSHEIM

Plant the Seed

I was making a retreat a few years ago when the priest directing me suggested I memorize and repeat this prayer several times a day:

> *Spirit of God, who dwells in all creation,*
> *I allow you to love me without reservation.*

Repeating this prayer was a powerful exercise. Eventually my mind was no longer saying words; my spirit was opening to God. Plant this seed in your own heart as you walk through these days of Lent and Easter.

Walking Through Lent

I think about Jesus going out to the desert for forty days and forty nights. The Lenten desert. And I wonder if I can also make a desert journey of these coming days and nights. I won't be able to leave the demands of my world, or be spared any of my responsibilities. I will have to listen to desert questions right in the midst of the city. Can I be that intentional?

My task this Lent is to listen with an open heart.

INDEX OPEN

As a test I leave work at noon to walk in the park, stopping to listen to the birds. Their song brings unexpected tears. I clear away stones and branches and rub dirt between my fingers. It is moist, this dust to which I will return. Even so, it reminds me of the fleetingness of everything. It reminds me that a light burns within and that I am charged with protecting that light. Through every difficulty, within each circumstance, this fire burns. Nothing harms me or tempts me apart from this presence. I let the fragrance of the trees penetrate my senses. In this quiet I know that I actually need very little, and want very little. This is what the desert is saying.

For these Lenten days I will allow the Spirit to raise questions and issues that are important for my journey. My task, to remain vigilant to everything I see. To listen. Just that would be enough if I could do it. To listen with an open heart to the Spirit within.

Allowing the Spirit to Guide Us

 We were following the route taken by Paul through Greece and Turkey. Every morning the group of twenty-five listened to the guide's itinerary for our day. I appreciated his sense of organization. But once the journey unfolded, it began to make less and less sense to me. Some mornings we covered a hundred miles, traveling east. Yet the very next morning we might travel two-hundred miles west, retracing our steps. This became a pattern. Finally I asked our guide why we were traveling in such an inefficient manner. He shrugged. "We're following the journey of Paul, exactly as he made it."

That felt even more confusing. Paul was traveling on foot. He would have thought things through. You would never add hundreds of miles to your journey by walking back and forth. You wouldn't backtrack. You would be careful. I expressed my bewilderment. The leader smiled. "You're thinking logically," he said. He emphasized that Paul would sometimes reach a town and realize he had left the previous village too hastily. Perhaps they still needed instruction. Or he might be hundreds of miles into the journey when he felt a call to return to the first church on his path. Remarkably, he listened. So the resulting zigzag pattern was the look of a journey led by the Spirit. I thought about my own life...my need for control, my goals. And beyond these, the possibility of a guidance from within that would be my eyes, and lead me.

Am I listening to the Spirit?

The Freedom of Our Deepest Self

I was a junior in high school, student of a beloved English teacher who was fair, but tough. If Mrs. Allen gave a good grade you knew you had earned it. She did not grade out of kindness, nor did she reward "potential." One weekend she asked our class to write a paper from the point of view of the King of England who had abdicated his throne for love.

A week later she walked between the rows putting the graded essays face down on each desk. As she laid my paper in front of me she paused and said, "Your essay made me cry." It wasn't much. Five words. I know I am a writer today because of that moment. I knew that her evaluation meant something.

In some respect we are always hoping for someone to see not only our talents, but our deepest self and the power it embodies. There are so many polite "no's" and "yes's" in our lives. In many ways we avoid the heart of things, and shy from what lies beneath the surface. Lending our lives to a deeper meaning and the emergence of truth is very different. It demands vigilance and commitment. It may involve choices that set us apart.

This is what's required to be "born again in spirit." From the heart of all things the Greater Soul asks us to pull our boats up on the beach, nets and all. Put those things aside. Follow me.

---

*Am I avoiding the heart of things,
the deeper meaning of truth?*

When Love Leads the Way

 The entrance to the Massachusetts State Prison for women was in full view. It was a spring evening, the moon full. I walked slowly toward the prison entrance wishing I had never accepted the chaplain's invitation to address a gathering of inmates. I grew acutely aware that the credentials I normally relied on—my license as a therapist, academic degrees, books I've written—would carry no weight here.

For more than fifteen years I'd led retreats and seminars. Those were comfortable settings. Now this new audience. What could I offer women largely illiterate, angry, despairing? I walked in with only a desire to help them find their way beyond hardship, and the story of how I had transformed my own pain.

That evening initiated me into the world of prisons—a world of deep longings and of broken hearts. A world of women taught by their life experience that they didn't matter. But not until I was inside the prison, confronted with faces and hearts, did I see how to reach them.

Life seems to follow this pattern: the journey unfolds as we live it out. My part is to let go with both hands and take the first step. The first step sets everything in motion. I think of Paul's journey through Greece and Turkey. Over a thousand miles on foot, searching for fertile hearts. Start walking, the Spirit demands. You're not alone. Love will lead the way.

Take the first step. You are not alone.

Come, Follow Me

Beside me is a glass of ice water. I'm sitting in a beach chair, but sitting inside, on a carpet, looking through a window at a maple tree. It's the magical morning hour when sunlight showers the tree's yellow leaves, then reaches further, its long arm entering my room, to create streaks and triangles across the floor. Tight slivers of light shaped by the window blinds shimmer and dance in front of me.

There is nothing else in my writing room but me, the beach chair, a sleeping bag, a thesaurus, the glass of water, and these patterns of light. But it is enough. Factoring in the tree and the light, it is more than enough.

I take periodic breaks from my work to read Joyce Rupp's account of her walk along the Camino road that stretches across Spain to the coast. The road winds under the Milky Way Galaxy toward Compostela, which means, literally, field of stars. For six weeks my friend walked with only a pack on her back and the openness in her heart.

In Louisiana I stood alongside hurricane evacuees who had only the shirts on their back. This same theme returns again and again to my life: we really need so little. Each day the spirit beckons. Will you come and follow me? Everything else is distraction from that outstretched hand.

How much do we really need?

Being Willing to Grow Up

 I sat on the floor of my bedroom closet holding my husband's bathrobe. He had been dead for four weeks. What is the meaning of life, I wondered? Was there value in the life I'd been living? Had I only lived to please others? My heartache was so deep. Was I brave enough to confront it?

Mark's Gospel reports that the disciples were at times filled with alarm. They were afraid. When Jesus walked on the water, they screamed and were terrified. They begged for explanations that weren't forthcoming. Everything was difficult, and they, like me, wanted it to be easy.

Now I was in a closet, immobilized. My life had never been harder.

Then a question presented itself: Are you willing to bear these circumstances in order to grow? Was I? Could I embrace the life that was mine? Could I embrace this fiery passage in order to search for something immoveable and true? Could I reach deep within and find the courage to change? Would I let love transform this pain into compassion and sight?

I found the difference that day between growing older, and really growing up. Scripture was no longer a story told of events long ago.

I heard the challenge to change my life spoken to my own soul. What I decided would determine my future.

Can I let love transform my pain
into compassion?

Clinging to Old Images

Food for thought: It was the demons and spirits who knew who he was; who recognized him. The people who surrounded him were only drawn by the signs and the wonders. The leaders of the day, those with the most to lose, those whose belief systems were the most fixed, called his words blasphemy. He ate with outcasts, and said that new wine had to be poured into fresh wineskins. Meanwhile the priests and elders made plans to kill him because he did not keep their version of the Sabbath and the law. The people said, "He has demons in him."

It's recorded that the disciples were often very afraid of him. Who is this man, they asked themselves? The wind and waves obey him, but the town of Nazareth rejected him, questioning his wisdom. Nothing about him fit their image of greatness. He fed five thousand people, but the disciples didn't understand the real meaning of it. "Their minds could not grasp it." Those three who witnessed the transfiguration were so frightened that they didn't know what to say.

"Forgive them, Father," he said, ultimately. "They don't know what they are doing." He said, "The things that are considered of great value by man are worth nothing in God's sight." These are the words I want to push away. These are the words that reveal how far I have to go.

What do I know about him?
How far do I have to go?

Being Aware of What Really Matters

 I knew her by chance, both of us scheduled to speak at the same conference hosted by a large religious organization. Her role was teaching church leaders how to assimilate new members, and her particular insights into human nature and group dynamics had a brush of genius. She was creative and engaging and everyone wanted her advice. Over a period of three or four years we found ourselves repeatedly at that same conference, and an easy friendship developed.

When she failed to appear in the fifth year I was disappointed. My phone call to her wasn't returned. Then I learned why. She was thirty-six, bright, with a brilliant life before her, and dying of cancer.

In the remaining months of her life she turned to friends for both solace and support. But in truth, it was she who supported them. She allowed conversations to be taped as friends posed questions, her clear, articulate style now focused on her imminent death, and what it had to teach about life. I listened to the tapes with great respect for her courage and clarity. One day a friend asked her what she might change, now that the divine force behind life was providing increasing awareness. She paused. "Knowing what I know now," she answered, "if I had my life to live over again, I wouldn't hurry. Not ever, for any reason. I would savor the brief hours."

Savor every day, every moment we are given.

Looking Past the Appearance of Things

 A bird sings at 5 AM. I will myself to my feet, pull on jeans and a t-shirt, and begin hiking with eleven other women through a camp in south Texas. Our path is strewn with fresh spider webs and dew, and the women ask if anything dangerous lurks in the shadows of scrub and bushes. Just pay attention, I say. At home, in northern Europe, they are respected teachers of science, government, math, and literature, but here the teacher is Nature.

Suddenly a single deer walks into the middle of the path, blocking our way. His flanks are heaving.

Look past appearances, I remind myself. We stop, breathing in rhythm with the deer's panting. When he wanders off we continue, each woman silent with private thoughts. But as we round the next bend the deer is there again, waiting, speaking without language.

In the presence of the deer, a fragile veil that separates me from a deeper awareness begins to shred. A woman whispers, "How is this possible, that a deer is causing me to feel different inside?" And in that split second, for a moment, I do not see a deer, but the Spirit that animates everything. The Spirit that sustains life is watching through creation. The Spirit moves invisibly in our midst. Then, just as quickly, the animal I've been watching is only a deer, and we go on.

Invisible in our midst,
the Spirit sustains life, all creation.

Asking Truer Questions of Life

 I see the way people behave differently when they begin to change. They ask different questions. They no longer ask, "why is God punishing me? Why did God do this to me?" They no longer announce, "I will never get over this. I will never forgive." They are more quiet, and thoughtful. They ask, "Can you help me accept and face this great challenge? Can you guide me past my bitterness? Can you show me how to stop giving away the gift of life to anger or resentment? Can you help me challenge myself to reach beyond fear?"

Every day I am creating who I am. My circumstances are not the architect of my life. I am. I can be courageous, if I choose to be. I can be self-disciplined. I can be responsible. I can refuse the grip of blame and hate. I can stand before my weaknesses, and fight.

My fears, perhaps, are only trying to awaken me to the true questions I need to ask.

Today I ask myself, "What good can be born in my life, affecting my family, my world?" What if I put aside my need to control, which has never brought me security or peace? In fact, when I cling to false securities, I throw away the opportunity to know myself at all. This day, I seek to know my true power. What is possible, if I am willing to live in a new way?

My circumstances are not
the architect of my life....I am.

Going Deeper into God

 Here in a strange city, facing a new crossroad, the realities of my life feel fierce. I'm longing for the beauty of familiar surroundings and a rich, predictable rhythm of work and love. But my path is ever changing. As soon as I root, life seems to uproot me. Each time I "hold on," life unwraps my fingers, sometimes with force. "I'm a gypsy," I bemoan to a friend. She laughs. "I like gypsies," she replies. But I won't be amused.

"Look at us," I say. "Our lives couldn't be more opposite. You're living in a world bursting with husband, children, homework, sports, and schedules. I live in airports and retreat centers. The faces before me each day are new." She calmly hands me a copy of an e-mail I'd written to her two years before. At that juncture I was nourishing a new relationship and her first husband had just died. It was she who observed, then, that our lives could not be more opposite. But I had disagreed. We are both doing the same thing, I'd written to her: Going deeper into God. Only the outer form is different.

Now my own words remind me that the outer appearance of things is what we call life, our means of being in the world. The inner effort pushing us to grow into the fullness of Spirit, is the soul's real journey.

It is the inner journey that really matters.

The Light Within

A beautiful, four-minute film captures faces of young and old persons all over the world. Some countenances are serious, some reflective, others joyous. Each race is represented. A first time viewer is usually caught up in the delight of human diversity—the many expressions of human life, the beauty of our sheer variety. Then the unforgettable last minute of the film begins to unfold. Now the filmmaker focuses on a particular face, especially the eyes, and as you are looking into those eyes, the eyes of another person emerge within that same gaze…and another, and yet another, until race, age, and gender blend and are superseded by spirit. You know that our apparent uniqueness is only a veil. There is a single truth, an inner nature, waiting to emerge in all life.

This force of spirit moves through circumstances, trying to make its presence known. It presses through to our hearts. "I've come to start a fire," Jesus announces. "How I wish it were blazing right now."

A fire of recognition, a fire of awakening. He looks at the woman getting water at the well. His gaze falls on the solitary figure being stoned. He watches a woman pour ointment on his feet. The same meaning is extended to each one. There's a purpose to everything you experience, it cries. Go beyond the surface of your life events, and let yourself hear a different voice calling you toward a true power that lies within.

Beneath the surface, the exterior, the artifice is where true meaning resides.

Secretly Made in the Depths of God

 How do we stop reinforcing the ideals of the culture that only create illusions, but do not bear truth? How do we stop clinging to thoughts that are barren? Among my own barren beliefs is the conclusion that I am a limited individual, and the events of my life are my life. But what if there is a knowledge much greater? What if I am much more than my personality? What if there is knowledge leading to freedom and joy? How will I know it?

The psalmist writes: You were secretly made and woven in the depths of God (Psalm 139). The words tell me that there is a truer nature within me…a true self. This nature precedes my birth and isn't bound by emotions, body, or mind. It is clear and free, the same substance as God—the same essential force of love.

How will I nourish this emerging inner self? How am I paying attention to the depth of God and to the potential of my being here? On the most basic level I begin to look at how I spend my hours. What do I read? What are my conversations? Do they foster the growth of something true, or am I only filling time? What changes am I willing to make to insure that the love that sustains me will make itself known?

How will I nourish this new emerging inner self?

Seeing the Holiness in the Ordinary

 I was in a rural village in Lithuania, being served a meal by an older woman who lived far from any city or conveniences. She had suffered hardship her whole life, yet she smiled at me tenderly, watching my eyes. She proudly picked up a pitcher of homemade apple juice and set it on the table, apple slices still floating in the liquid. She watched me as I drank her nectar. Then she set a china bowl of stew in front of me. I was aware that providing this meal had cost her dearly, and aware at the same moment that the meal was incidental. The force of love reaching out through her was the true meal.

If we've been taught to look for God only in scriptures, churches, or the lives of the saints, we will not pay attention to something real that is right before us. Instead, we will safeguard the images of God we were given as children, and ignore anything outside of those parameters.

Seeing what is true demands expanded vision. Like the disciples, we are called to let go of expectations and images and respond to something deep within our own hearts. Guided by this inner love, we begin to find our way. That same love led me to the seemingly simple meal in the small village.

When I finished the stew we sat quietly. My friend said very few words. It was more than enough just to sit at her table.

Let go of expectations and respond to the call
deep within your heart.

The Nature of Fear

 I'd invited a group of women to experience a beautiful spot on the far side of a bluff in the high desert of the southwest. I promised to guide them one by one along a well-marked trail, although the last half-mile required leaving the trail to follow me through thick brush. I agreed to return at a set time to lead them back safely.

Some women were afraid of the height of the bluff, others feared the wildlife or being alone outside for several hours. The challenge demanded that they trust me, the terrain, and themselves.

As I left the marked trail with the first woman, her pace slowed. When I could no longer hear her footsteps I looked back. She was standing beside a tree tearing pieces of tissue into small pieces, then laying them carefully on the branches. I remembered the fairy tale, Hansel and Gretel. The tissue was her bread trail. Her way back home, in case I didn't come.

I was witnessing the nature of fear. Gripped by fear, I've sometimes stayed in dim rooms and dark corners when the power of a bluff awaited me. Because of fear I've clung to traditions that bound me, and have fallen into a web of repetitious patterns that brought me no joy. I never saw, as I wandered in those dark and lonely spaces, that freedom was one step away, or that the Spirit within could lead me to larger places.

Under the grip of fear,
we are unaware of the Spirit within.

A Power Beyond Fear

 No infant approaches life consciously thinking, "I'll resist the life held out to me. I'll cling to anger and fear. I'll choose not to let life impact my heart. I'll live afraid of taking risks, afraid to challenge myself. I'll create a safe and familiar pattern, no matter how limited, and defend it with my every action."

Similarly, no one stands at the beginning of a relationship and says, "I think I'll hurt you. I think that I, above all others, will fail to see who you really are. You, whom I profess to love, I will one day punish by withholding access to my heart." And yet, human life easily unfolds this way. Afraid to become who we truly are, we reach out tentatively, or not at all.

According to Jesus, there is something within us that is greater than fear. It has nothing to do with religion; it has to do with God. Raw God. There is nothing to learn about this God. No knowledge to acquire. Nothing to believe. It's a matter of paying attention to the Spirit within. Of opening a door. A willingness to know who we truly are.

Who would I be and what power would be expressed through my life if I were not dominated by fear?

Released from the clutches of fear,
what could I become?

Love Is Everywhere, Trying to Break In

He went walking by the Sea of Galilee and he saw fishermen casting their nets into the sea. "Follow me," he said. But he came disguised as Beauty and Treachery and Delight and Loneliness and Adversity, and Power and Mystery and Longing. He came disguised as the universe. Disguised as my life, and yours. And he said, "I can transform all that has happened to you, and all that you are. I can cure the sickness in your heart. I can teach you to see. I can show you that love is everywhere, trying to break in."

"Would you like to learn what life is? Then let me show you how to come up against your fear. It's possible because I stand outside the door of your heart. I am still moving. Creation is ongoing. Are you yet willing to move with me? I am the fire that leads the way through the darkness. I fill you with visions and dreams. I call you forward. Can you transcend what you already know and let me teach you more? Can you put down the tenets of faith protected by your ancestors and let me call you forth in new ways? It is I, who stands outside your door."

Will you allow love to enter,
to transform your heart?

A Daily Practice

 Hiking in the mountains I find time to look at myself. What sound is my life making, I wonder? What is the speed of my life? Is there ever silence? Or enough silence? A silence that is true listening, not merely the absence of noise while I still fill the minutes with activity? I know a plant won't grow without water. Am I watering my spirit in the way that matters? Someone suggested that it would be shocking to view your own life, like a movie, but without words. To simply watch yourself, to see how you've chosen to spend the hours of a day. More difficult, perhaps, to see the hours you've missed. Hours that sped by, filled with concerns of so little consequence. The fleeting beauty never noticed.

I decide to make one small change. I will incorporate one new action to counterbalance the busyness that surrounds me. I begin a daily practice of reading a poem. I read slowly, savoring the images. A friend with whom I share this idea begins a daily practice of her own. She begins to step outside every evening to drink in the sky above. There is power in a small change. The power of an inner door flung open. The delight of sudden sweetness when you find a new world within you, where God was waiting all along.

There is a sweetness and power
when you discover God within you.

Peace and Freedom Lie Within

I imagine a classroom for those about to be born. A "pre-birth class," of sorts, where vital instructions are given:

You'll be born to certain parents in a particular geographical region.

You'll have differing talents and varying advantages and disadvantages. Eventually this "story," the story of your history, will be very compelling. It will grow and take over, and you will lose yourself in it. This precise means of having a life and living on Earth will appear to be the meaning of life, no longer just a vehicle for being here. The speed of life will also take over. The whole point of your journey is to awaken to the Spirit within, but you won't remember that. You'll believe it's about getting married, raising children, achieving milestones, getting enough food to eat. Still, the work of the Spirit continues, an unbreakable thread weaving through life. Within the context of your story you will, at times, face adversity, but on the invisible level of Spirit something strong and powerful will be emerging. Ironically, your circumstances may seem most dark when you are actually closest to this awakening.

Beauty will assist you. Also, order. Love. Silence. You will have access to a strength and power greater than anything you face. But you must know this, and be willing to turn toward it. The peace and freedom you seek will always lie within.

The whole point of our journey is to awaken the Spirit within us.

SHUTTERSTOCK

The Peace of God

 I was in Washington D.C. to attend a gala at the Kennedy Center, but had arrived a day early in order to spend the morning at Rock Creek Cemetery. I'd been told there was an exquisite sculpture within those sprawling grounds entitled, The Peace of God. Finding the sculpture was not peaceful. It took two cab drivers and great persistence to find the right entrance to the cemetery, let alone to locate the art. But two hours later, I was sitting before it, the turmoil of getting there a distant memory.

My friend was right. Somehow, seeping through the stone, was a great feeling of well being and hope for mankind. A great sense that we live within the embrace of a love we little know. I thought of the lines attributed to Julian of Norwich, "And all shall be well."

That evening I attended the gala. A crush of glamorous stars and VIP politicians filled the aisles, the din of their voices dissonant and unsettling after the power of the morning. I finally ducked outside to get air and found a bench underneath the real stars. The contrast between the morning stillness and the evening revelry could not have been more distinct. Thirteen-year-old Holocaust victim, Anne Frank, wrote in her diary, "The best remedy for those who are…lonely or unhappy is to go outside, somewhere where they can be quiet, alone with the heavens…." Somewhere to know the peace of God.

Outside, in the embrace of nature,
we can feel the presence of God.

Living As the Light of the World

 This morning I pray for the human race. For friends, scattered in every country and continent. For tribes who have never left their forest. For prisoners of war, famine, fear, terror. Even the drunk driver who hit our car, killing my loved ones. We stand together, each of us. Shoulder to shoulder. Heart to heart. I look at the human race and feel its travail.

In my lifetime I will physically stand beside very few of the billions of us who occupy planet Earth at this time in history. Most of us will never be in the same space at the same time. I accept that. But what will I do with the ones whose lives do touch mine?

According to Scripture, we are the salt of the earth, the light of the world. A friend tells me about her five-year-old grandson, an active, rambunctious boy. On a recent boat trip, he announced that he needed some alone time, and sat by himself at the bow of the boat. It was so uncharacteristic that his mother asked three times if he was all right. He said that the gods were talking to him and refused to say more. A day later, she asked what they had told him. He said, "They told me, never, never, never, NEVER hurt anyone."

The words of the gods through the five-year-old boy are penetrating. What would it mean to literally live in that way?

Never, never hurt anyone.

The God Who Holds Us

 I stood on a dirt road with a twelve-year-old girl, both of us looking up, watching a nest of baby storks. The stork parents had just signaled for the babies to fly for the first time and our hearts were beating fast. It was an aerial nest perched atop a fifty-foot pole. Three of the five babies immediately took flight, wings flapping clumsily. But still, they were flying. We watched them make small circles in the air, confidence growing with each minute aloft. The remaining two birds moved to the edge, peered out, and remained frozen.

For several minutes the parent stork clicked its beak and flew backwards, encouraging the babies to leave. Nothing. Then an older man, walking on the path, looked up and whispered compassionately to the babies, "Don't be afraid. All you have to do is open your wings. The wind will do the rest." In the next moment, as we watched, the babies timidly spread their wings and left the safety of the nest. The wind carried them.

Such a simple, beautiful moment. It stayed with me that night and into the next day. Just spread your wings. There is something beneath you, little bird. There is something holding you, little soul. Don't be afraid.

Don't be afraid. There is something beneath you.

God, Show Us Who You Are

 Sitting in my new apartment, I was brokenhearted, alone, and without hope, too weary to go on. I had survived the accident that killed my family, but would I survive the pain created by the loss? Would my heart ever open again to life, knowing the potential of life to wound? Seven months pregnant, I grimaced at the irony: Death all around me, life within me. Which force would win?

God was clearly not the God I wanted God to be. I wanted a God who stopped speeding cars. I wanted a God who could be counted on to protect us. Once, a friend told me about driving in his car, his knuckles white on the steering wheel, reeling from news he didn't want to face. "God," he seethed, "I'm going to fight this with everything I have." From within came the knowing, *I am all you have.*

This night it was me who was seething. I wanted a miracle. I wanted answers. I wanted my old life back. I wanted to be carefree. This was not how I imagined my twenties. But only one prayer found its way to my lips. "God, show me who you are." I had no way of understanding the power of that unfeigned reaching out. That night I came to God with all my heart. In my own way I said, You are all I have. I only know that within that surrender the first gleam of light appeared.

In my own way, you are all I have.

The Mystery of God

 Scientists report that every one of the stars is a sun, and some suns are so large they could contain the sun and the earth and the distance between them. Even greater, it is estimated that there are over one hundred million galaxies, and that this universe expands at the rate of two million miles a second. It is not physics. The hand of God created this.

I walk outside in the dark and look up. You created this, I say, and I have trivialized you. I've heard myself say, "God wants this," or "God thinks that." "This is God's will." I hope in those moments your compassion was wide. How we strut! We even announce that we are "saved," and judge whether or not others are as fortunate. Ah, our little ego, presuming to even glimpse this knowledge. One bolt of lightening reminds me. Merely the glare of your face blinds me forever. It is not from my ego or mind that I will ever know you.

Mystery is who you are. Holy, sacred mystery. Divine mystery. Terrible, wonderful, incomprehensible, beyond words, beyond thought, mystery. Greater than the mind. Infinitely greater than our hubris. I do not even breathe apart from your power. And even though I often pretend otherwise, I do not know anything until you change my inner sight. I stand beneath the starlight and watch.

We cannot breath apart
from God's power and mystery.

Encountering the Living God

 Do I really listen to new ideas with a heartfelt openness to grow? I appear receptive, but aren't I simply taking in and confirming what I already believe, and nothing more? Fixed in my world view, insulated from change, I protect myself, creating a fail safe way to cling to the security of a comfortable life.

If the first disciples had had a similar mind set, they would never have followed. It's sobering to say that. Their enormous "yes" required unreasonable and unparalleled openness to change. In the end, it was their willingness to suspend cherished beliefs that served them.

Why does the path challenge ideals, tearing apart our deepest religious conclusions? Why does God demand our stubborn wills? I'd rather a God who fits my own image of God, a God who doesn't turn tables (and lives) upside down. Why does encountering the living God allow confusion to enter my life? Or turmoil? Why must I be responsible for what I've been shown?

This is why I want the Easter story to remain a story about other people living in a different time. Let God break through their pretenses, not mine. Let the Divine exchange their illusions and ideals for real knowledge, and leave me untouched. Yet my fear is that I am one of the people in that story. That the story is ongoing, and they modeled a way we must all go.

Am I open to an encounter with God?

The Pursuit of God

A print of two picture frames is in front of me, sent by friends in honor of their sixtieth wedding anniversary. In the first frame is their wedding photo, both bride and groom expectant and new; in the second frame, the same couple, sixty years later. Looking at both frames, I imagine that experiences and challenges they never anticipated in the earlier years nevertheless intruded, and colored their lives indelibly. Some choices they were forced to make probably closed one door and opened another.

Almost certainly the long path they've actually walked wasn't what they expected it to be. We all learn this. Marriage isn't what we expect. Growing older isn't what we expect. Our children don't become who we imagined them to be. The actual journey is a surprise.

Somewhere within the long life represented by those two frames, I imagine that they each faced a personal garden of Gethsemane. I'm sure they experienced fear in that garden. And pain. They had to decide whether or not to surrender to the Soul who beckoned them. This moment, of course, was not photographed. It could not be captured. It is only visible in the beauty and power of their lives. It is only evident in the pursuit of God with all your heart.

Our journey will be filled with surprises, challenges, Gethsemanes.

INDEX OPEN

What Do You Really Want?

 What do you want? Jesus asked over and over again. What do you want me to do for you? And along the way someone answered, I just want to see.

One night in a shelter I was speaking with fifty women marked by long suffering. Some looked at me, but a few kept their heads down, using a hand to shield their faces so they couldn't be seen. I spoke to them for a little while, and then asked them to speak to me. That's when the power in the room shifted. Their stories were unrelenting litanies of severe hardship and deprivation. They had suffered abandonment, deceptions, rapes, beatings,…and deaths, often multiple deaths. They told tales of running away, and long, desperate searches for someone, anyone, to provide love. And yet, with a thousand strikes against them, still, the courage to keep going on, one day at a time. We cried together.

One woman took my hand as I said goodbye. "Don't forget us," she said. "Pray for us. Because I saw tonight that I can still love. Love was in me all along." I don't remember her face, but I remember how her courage made me feel. I remember thinking that she would find what she wanted, because she wanted it so deeply.

Amid the suffering, we search for love.

The Hidden God

 Every longing is for God. Every love is about the Divine. Lift the veil on any human drama, on any addiction, and there is God, reaching to us. In one disguise or another, there is God saying, "Come."

There is God saying, "Can you not spend this one hour with me? Can you not stay awake?" The very moment you are about to take casually is filled with light.

How simple, unassuming and ordinary are our lifetimes. How unmatched is the power of seeing beauty in precisely what we've been given. In realizing that no other circumstance is better, or preferable. In knowing the mere glory of a day. In understanding that the Divine for whom our souls long lies hidden in the smallest corner.

I remember when the Berlin wall was dismantled and a great euphoria erupted. There was a sense of unspeakable freedom, an unleashed force of hope. The world momentarily believed that everything is possible, and goodness might win. But soon the realities of re-building economic systems appeared, and also the challenge of uprooting tenacious beliefs. The iron strongholds of the mind and its long-held perceptions were stronger than any outer wall. Replacing ideals with real visions of truer selves and deeper natures was a challenge for the bravest. And it is our challenge, still. I ask myself, "Can I stay awake? Can I look into this day ahead, and see, within the disguise of events and circumstances, the shimmering light?"

In one way or another,
God beckons us to come to him.

Changed by the Hand of God

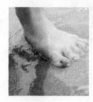 It's early afternoon and I am sitting around a circular wooden table with a group of young teenagers in Eastern Europe. They watch eagerly as I teach them to cut and fold greeting cards until a small box is created. They are astonished when the box emerges, and then eagerly reach for cards in order to create boxes of their own.

The next morning one young girl pulls several beautiful questions from her box:

Who can tell me what the sweet bird speaks to the oak?
Where are our dreams going?
Where is the sun spending the night?

How many questions like this have been asked since the beginning of time? Yet no true question is answered, no one sees what they have never seen before, without first being radically changed. I am reminded of the Scripture where Jesus told Peter to walk on the water. We all face the boat and the water and that command, "Step out of the boat." The waves have to lap over our ankles. We have to let go of the very things we cannot live without. We have to set aside our images, our conclusions, our prejudices, and our rightness. We have to be astonished. Then, from that place of willingness and trust, we feel the rocking motion of the water and begin to walk toward something true.

Be willing to trust, 'Step out of the boat.'

The Courage to Face Your Life

I had begun to run. Not with any real passion, or promise. But my daily walk now included spurts of running…at least until the breath drained out of me and I couldn't go on. Then I walked and gasped until I regained normal breathing and summoned the wherewithal to run for yet another quarter mile. As I disciplined myself to this new routine I felt increasingly smug. This is good, I said, congratulating myself. Look at me.

A few months into my running my father had a debilitating stroke. We hung on the doctor's words, anxious about his loss of speech, and the paralysis on his left side. The road back would be long. He was a heavy man, elderly. The physical therapy would demand all his resolve. It was painstaking to watch his slow progress. To watch the aides massage his muscles until his legs were stronger. To see him finally stand up for the first time. To witness the tremendous will he summoned before he took a first step.

I was there the day he took one-hundred-fifty steps without stumbling. Then he sat and wept. He had made his way to the piano he could no longer play. My running was put into such perspective by my father's slow, determined recovery. Sometimes there is only the center of God's will, and your own "yes."

Often it takes all our willpower to summon
the courage to take the first step.

Offering Back Our Lives

 There's something about the baptism of Jesus in the river. Not the crowds, nor the dove. Not the voice from the heavens, or the wild, radical forerunner, the one who prepared the way. It's the power of "turning in" your old life, and stepping into a freedom that was always there. A moment when you refuse to be content to rearrange your life one more time. You finally weigh the pain of seeing against the pain of not seeing. The pain of loving against the pain of not loving. You take your fingers off the compass point and become new.

An Episcopal bishop from Uganda was visiting in the states this winter, and I met him briefly. He attended a performance of my play, "On My Way Home," which tells the story of the death of my family, and my own subsequent road to healing. I was deeply moved by the bishop's presence, since his own spouse and daughter had been violently killed in Uganda. His intolerable pain was visible in the great black pools behind his eyes.

He took my hands following the performance. "I realized tonight that in the end, every step is about surrender. A lifetime of surrendering, each surrender following the next. But eventually, we either will or won't offer back our lives."

The reflection was his, but I heard it as my own. Why do I cling to ideas that limit me? Who or what do I really serve?

Every step is a form of surrender.

Making Peace with Change

In a story called The Giver, written by Lois Lowry, the author creates a perfect world. No fear. No pain. No choices.

Everyone follows the rules, and everything is of equal importance. As a result, there is no happiness. There is sameness. Just one person in that society remembers a time when life encompassed beauty and diversity, but he holds these memories alone.

The reader vicariously experiences life as we often say we wish it could be: predictable, without change, loss, or pain. Nothing unsettling exists. But neither does the spectacular movement of the animating Spirit. There is no expression of God.

College students once asked me for solid, practical advice as they wrestled with events that had brought great upheaval into their lives. I responded, "Make peace with change." My friend's mother says it best: "In the face of sadness remember, this too will pass. In the face of happiness remember, this too will pass."

All circumstances are transient. Only from within will you find the unchanging, immovable source of equanimity and peace. The beauty and order of God isn't found in sameness and stasis. The very nature of Spirit is characterized by diversity. All life is becoming.

Learn to accept change. All life is becoming.

Life, The Greatest Gift

The town in Europe where I am staying was founded in 1338. I walk toward a small stone church on a path that others have walked for six centuries. Elderly men and women ride by on bicycles, milk pails swinging from the handlebars. An old woman sweeps her front steps with tree branches tied with twine. The scent of roses is everywhere.

At night I listen to the stories of these villagers, remembrances of fearful years lived under a communist occupation. Outwardly they learned to appear faithful to the government's avowed atheism, safety depending upon this pretense. Children were taught to repeat the lies as well. But their hearts and souls knew differently, and at Easter they closed the curtains and spoke truth in whispers. Held it close, as a jewel.

"How did you keep joy alive?" I ask. It is the question of the daughter of middle class parents, one who has always had enough to eat and grew up free and unafraid. The mother with whom I am speaking watches me. "When you see the value of being alive," she says slowly, "when you know the value of life itself—there is joy." She smiles. "Life is the greatest gift," she tells me. She shifts, as if she is about to say more. Instead, she folds her hands and drops her eyes, letting the deepest meaning of her words find their way to my heart.

I wonder: Do I value what I say I value?

When you know the value of life, there is joy.

The Sheer Miracle of Life

 Before me are photographs taken by astronauts and cosmonauts as they orbited the earth and landed on the moon. From that distance the earth shrinks in size, appearing fragile. The image of a blue-white earth rising like a crescent over our own moon is particularly breathtaking. I'm aware of how fixed I am to my every day vision, and how ill accustomed to this perspective of watching earth from space.

The astronauts comment that when viewed from space it is evident that Earth is mostly water. The land masses on which we live are the least of Earth. A Soviet cosmonaut adds another perspective. He remembers when their ship was flung into deep space, it seemed like there was no power that could ever bring the ship back. The darkness seemed too great.

Yet Earth, so immediate, the very rock beneath us, doesn't appear to be mostly water, or hung in darkness, unconnected to anything. "We are floating through [a] deep black void" (Edgar Mitchell). A stunning photograph makes it clear. Our sheer existence is miracle.

Some photos capture extraordinary frames of thunder. Lightening. The frail line of horizon, sunrise seen from space, and then, in contrast, the majesty of the Northern Lights. In the presence of such radiance something within us stirs. A recognition. But even more than that, a longing.

Even viewed from the firmament, life is a miracle.

Changing Our Consciousness

 She was a young mother with three children when her husband was killed. In front of her were seemingly endless tasks, all begging her attention. The weight of life was keen. Day by day she fought her way through the sorrow, comforting her children and crying alone at night. Then after a year passed she packed up her family and went to live in Nairobi for several months. It was a chance to experience a totally different culture, to utilize her skills in photography, and perhaps to know herself in a new way. To begin again.

One morning while in Africa she was looking at a catalog from the states, making decisions about some jackets for the children and a sweater for herself. A native came to her door to say hello and asked what she was doing. Opening the catalog, she showed him the picture of the sweater she was preparing to order. A puzzled and confused expression spread over the man's face. Assuming that mail-order must be an unfamiliar concept in the small village, she asked what was wrong. "Why," he wanted to know, "would you buy a second sweater when you are already wearing one that is in perfect condition?"

In relating this experience to me five years later, she confessed that the question posed to her that day still dominates her life. Now I hear the force of his question myself. If we are truly one spirit, one body, don't we have to look differently at how we live, and love, and use the resources of this world?

What is our responsibility to God's creation?

What Do I Truly Value?

Years ago I took voice lessons from an acclaimed musician. He was well-known and highly regarded for his talents, and the lessons were a generous gift. At the time we were both on the faculty of the same college.

I scheduled these lessons in between appointments with my counselees, and once or twice in a row I was a few minutes late in arriving. I could have been on time, actually, but the first time I stopped to speak briefly with another faculty member, the second time I delayed to make a phone call that wasn't critical. The third time I was a few minutes tardy my friend said to me, "If you were paying for this hour, you wouldn't be late."

The words stung. I knew he was right and I instantly saw that my tardiness reflected the value I placed on the opportunity he was offering. I felt ashamed, and was never late again. I did value the gift.

Sometimes I remember that moment in regards to my own inner journey. I hear a voice in a whisper, "If you really saw the gift of life you've been given, you wouldn't throw it away." It jolts me from a preoccupation with a thousand peripheral things. It makes me aware of how my default position in life easily becomes my comfort, my ease, my desire to be appreciated and loved. Against this is the gaze of a man in the desert asking for a friendship from which I am too often estranged.

What is the value of the opportunity offered?

The Power in Our Lives

 I listen to the sound of spring rain soaking grasses already filled with pools of wet life. The power of water and wind is very real to me. But as I hear the rhythmic drops against the window, I am not thinking about nature's power, but about the power that fills me—the power contained in all our lives. I remember my thirty-minute visit with a wise old man, long ago, who told me I was alive for a reason, and to go out and find it. It was so tempting to hear his challenging words and dismiss them. To just go on with the busyness of my life. The world's power is compelling, and God's voice quiet in comparison.

It was a lot to think about. Building walls around my life is easy. I know how to live in regret. I am expert at recapturing a past experience, refusing to let it go. But if I decide that one or two things or people are the only things that give meaning to my life, isn't there something much more serious to face?

I watch the storm and wonder if I will ever pour out all that I am. Will I live spilled out, or choose to live cautiously? I can't change the past; I can change this moment. Twenty years from tonight, what sound will my life have made?

Will I live spilled out or choose caution?

What We Were Created to See

 I'd spent several days at a cottage in the woods, wandering and hiking until my legs would carry me no further. Some mornings I sat on stones and looked into the distance for hours letting the morning mist soak through. I watched the sun rise and watched it set. I followed the moon through the night sky. I also befriended one particular deer—a doe. One evening she stood behind me as dusk approached. When I moved to a different stone, for a different vantage, she followed me. So I picked up one leg, very slowly and quietly, and stomped three times in the dirt. She imitated me. I stomped two times. She stomped twice. I did it once. She followed. Finally I bowed to her and she stared straight into my eyes until I knew I'd been looked right through.

I've read that truth is never expressed in words. Truth is sighted suddenly. In her eyes I saw that life is a banquet. We live in a garden. The kingdom is now. But I don't live day to day with that deepest knowledge. I fall asleep. Wake up, wake up, wake up the mystics and prophets say. Wake up, says the doe. See what you were created to see.

Truth is never expressed in words.

Seeing Beauty in All I've Been Given

 It was hard, accepting changes I did not want. I thought my husband and daughter were mine. But they weren't. They were gifts. And when I began to see them as gifts, it began to change. A gift and a possession are treated so differently. I had wanted security and comfort and guarantees, and until they died I had the illusion that I had them. But life is not about keeping things. It is about having eyes for beauty and learning to let go.

A little bit at a time I began to hope. I took ordinary steps. I looked at my life. Life is not safe and it is not always fair. Love is a risk. But it is still beautiful. I saw that bitterness and anger must be nourished in order to stay alive. I stopped nourishing them, and started to nourish me. It was a choice. I stopped moving against life, and began to move with it. I let it teach me. It happened slowly. Deciding to see beauty in what I was given was a difficult choice.

I moved from learning "about" God to experiencing God. I saw that the world labors to open its heart, just as I was trying to open mine. I saw that the things that happened to me could teach me, and broaden my perspective. Through the ordinary events of my life God was calling to me. Get out of the boat. Walk. The seas will hold you.

A gift and a possession are so different.

What Do I Really Reverence?

Today's gospel recalls the exhilarating approach to Jerusalem. The palm lined streets. The joy of (seeming) victory. But great triumph is never isolated. Everything in life is balanced by its eventual destruction. Can we truly live twenty, thirty, forty years, and not see that? Everything is temporary, and we are "entitled" to nothing. Life is given freely. All our needs are provided for. Water to live. Plants and animals for our nourishment. Flowers for beauty. Trees to shade, shelter us. Stones to provide our homes. Gems to delight our hearts. But we possess none of it. It is ours to use as we are passing through...walking by, as they walked the path to the shining city on a hill.

So how do we hold what is so fleeting? With respect. With appreciation for what we are given. With gratitude for the things we have known, even briefly. With reverence. I ask myself, "Am I open and clear? Do I choose what is beautiful? Do I discipline myself to live in a balanced way? Would I have lined the road to Jerusalem with palm fronds? Would I have joined the march, scuffing along the dusty roadway? What do I reverence enough to follow it with my life?"

What do I reverence enough to follow it with my life?

INDEX OPEN

43

Insist upon pretense, and you'll have it. Insist upon mediocrity, and it is yours. Insist upon beauty and you will find it. Insist upon learning, and you will learn. Insist upon living with great passion, and you will see differently. You will not merely "join a mob," marching to a distant city. You will walk because you must. Because there is no other response. Because you have been given so much, and love impels you to go.

Five Loaves and Two Fishes

 What dream was alive in you when you were young? With those words a priest asks a group of us to introduce ourselves. We listen with respect to one another's dreams until the conversation threads its way around the room a second time, and we are asked how many of us have actually lived out the pursuit of those dreams. Only two out of twelve have done so.

I let the awareness settle in. One of the seminal lessons of my own grief (at age twenty-seven my husband and oldest daughter were killed in an accident with a drunk driver), was that life may not go the way you wanted it to. Your original dreams may shatter. You may be asked to find beauty and hope in ways you never imagined.

Both then and following the group experience, I walked away sobered by the power and mystery of life…the many forks in the road. The destinies that have to be redesigned or relinquished. The choices that we make and the choices that are made for us. That night I wrote in my journal: Five loaves and two fishes. Every day I have five loaves and two fishes. This is what I have to work with. Whether or not they are the loaves and fishes I intended is outside of my control. Whether or not there is a feast is up to me.

What are the dreams you have deferred?

Finding a Greater Love

 In the depth of grief over the loss of my family, I saw how I was clinging to things. I'd thought my family members were mine. I thought they belonged to me. I let them become my purpose for living, scarcely realizing what I was doing. It was subtle and acceptable. Everyone lived this way. But in the throes of grief there slowly emerged a greater clarity. Many illusions began to be unveiled.

Now nothing mattered except discovering whether or not life had a truer purpose. If not, then what was the point of going on?

Through eyes so newly open I recognized a force of love at work trying to show me a completely different order of things. Apart from the purpose I wanted or had created for my life, there was a larger meaning. The gift of life is enormous. Something was trying to awaken me to a greater love that reached beyond my private concerns and encompassed so much more. I didn't have to cling to things or be afraid. Love was leading the way.

At the time, this awareness appeared to be a small shift, an insignificant distinction. But, in fact, it was a great key. The secret of life is not embedded in any single outcome. Simple lives have great power if we are able move past our own desires. When I listened for the larger movement of Spirit, I began responding to my own soul.

Even simple lives can have great power.

Am I Yet Open to Love?

 I say, "I love you," and imagine an emotion welling up from within. But truly, love originates from a reality that is not my own. The love that takes form in my nature is not "my" love. Love already exists. The question is: Is there an opening in me that allows love to take form and character in my nature?

For years I lived holding onto anger, instead of letting love rise up in me. I did it with my father. He'd withdrawn himself from his family, but now, as an adult, I had the authority to forgive him, and let love be the final say. Instead, I continued to judge him. Then one night, driving in my car, I asked God how to turn my judgments into love before my father died.

Gratitude was the answer. Gratitude. So I said, "Thank you" out loud. I thanked my father for my life, and for the fact that we did what we could with our relationship. There was too much hurt, but still, "Thank you." Thank you. My eyes filled with tears. For the first time I saw the soul that is my father, and wanted it to soar. I realized that it must have been wretched living so many years, unable to show love. Thank you. I glanced up at the crescent moon. Has my father ever loved the night, as I do? Did the crescent moon ever catch his breath? God, I hoped so.

If we loved, imagine how strong the world would be.

Love exists. Show it freely.

Nothing Exists Apart from God

What do you know for certain? The question, posed by a friend, was challenging, and answering wasn't as easy as I'd thought. There are many things I believe. Things I hope. Things I've been taught. But what do I know for certain?

Even the darkness is held by light. I scratched the words onto a page and looked at them. Even the darkness is held by light. Yes, I know this most of all. There is no corner of creation, no event, no circumstance where God is not. There is no life, period, apart from the Spirit. In my own most penetrating darkness, my husband and daughter senselessly killed, still…there was light. Whether or not I saw it, whether or not I believed…light penetrated my life. God is found in the depths of both the light and the dark.

Lent reminds me of this deeper knowing: The universe is ordered to God. And I must learn to see beyond passing disappointments and accept the exquisite timing of creation and of my own journey. Where I listen to life from is crucial. From ego, the gratification of my own needs and satisfactions takes over. From ego, my circumstances dominate, and the dark appears to be separate from God.

But looking from the spirit within, I know differently. I know that everything unfolds in its time. I know that within all adversity is a force of love that prevails. I am safe, even in the dark.

*What do
we really know
for certain?*

TRIDUUM

Eyes to See

For years I spent Holy Week on retreat with a small community, happily tucked into my cell of a room for eight days. In the evenings we all came together for Mass and brief rituals. There were also evenings of vigil, and over the years, against my best intentions, I often fell asleep when I was supposed to be awake and in prayer.

Could you not keep awake just one hour?

DESIGN PICS

TRIDUUM

50

One year on Holy Thursday something nudged me awake at 3 AM telling me to get out of bed and go to the chapel. But I overruled the feeling and stayed warm inside my covers. The next evening a fellow retreatant named David said he'd been in the chapel at 3 AM desperately praying for someone else to wait with him. I didn't know what to say.

On Good Friday we went to a field to walk the Stations of the Cross and remember the walk to Golgotha. David spoke about the Roman centurion who'd stood at the foot of the cross. He entered the heart of that centurion and imagined the words his spirit might have spoken if he'd suddenly understood at whose feet he stood.

I barely remember David's words. What I do remember was the look in his eyes and then him shaking with tears as he imagined himself right into that man, and felt himself overtaken by sight. Actually, there was no imagination involved. He was, in that moment, a man overtaken by sight. There will never be words to describe it.

Being Love for One Another

I was exhausted, hungry, and out of sorts. I had just cleared customs in Atlanta after a series of flights from Europe that caused me to miss a full night's sleep. Now the flight to get me back home from Atlanta was delayed. I had another six hours to wait. I went to my gate area, delighted to find it empty.

Wrapping my backpack straps around my legs, I was just about to stretch out across three chairs and try to sleep when a very elderly lady pushing a wheelchair approached me. She was bone weary, confused…looking for her gate and a flight to Charleston to visit her daughter. I pulled myself up from my temporary bed with supreme effort, sighed, helped the woman get into the wheelchair, and started walking, looking for video monitors that would help us figure out where she needed to be. The monitor, at least a ten-minute walk away, showed that her flight had already left. It was the last flight to Charleston that evening. I forgot my own weariness.

What on earth was she going to do? Then I asked to see her ticket. Her eyes filled up. She'd lost the ticket. In her purse was an envelope that read, "Mother's Ticket." But the ticket wasn't there. I trudged on, ten more minutes of walking until we found an Information booth. There was a long line, but leaning on the edge of the booth was a young, male flight attendant, ready to go home, his shift over. He caught my eye and smiled. "What's wrong?" he asked. I explained. He looked at the sweet woman in the wheelchair, almost asleep. Looked at me. Then looked right into me. "I think," he said slowly, "I think you've done your part. I think the rest is up to me. I won't leave her, I promise you. Even if she needs a room for the night, I won't leave her until she gets on a plane for Charleston."

I said goodbye to the woman and turned to watch them wheel down the walkway. I watched until they were out of sight. Then I returned to my makeshift bed in my own gate area, but I couldn't lie down. The image of the attendant and the woman was still too strong. I stared straight ahead. It's so easy, I sat there thinking. So easy.

It was a very simple encounter, on the surface. Someone who was elderly needed assistance. Help was provided. But it was the way this young man had responded—looking right into my eyes. He engaged something inside of me. In that look, we were no longer passenger, elderly woman, and flight attendant. We were three human beings whose paths had momentarily crossed. He took it seriously: We are here for one another. And in that moment of love, he changed my evening. Bettered it. Showed me the way home to a different home.

Is it too great a stretch to surmise that in just such a way Simon helped with the cross, and Veronica wiped a man's bleeding face? When love overtakes us, our own presence in this world wields great power. This is the power beyond death; the love for which so much was given.

Christ revealed the gift of love, a power beyond death.

TRIDUUM

DESIGN PICS

Easter

History records that on the way to his death, a woman wiped the face of Jesus. When I think of wiping someone's face, I think of wiping the face of one of my children. Touching them. It is an intimate act.

When I first saw the AIDS quilt, years ago, I felt so close to the stories and lives it represented that my hand involuntarily reached out to touch the cloth. I rolled the velvet from someone's jacket between my fingers, the jacket now permanently sewn onto a square of the quilt. Next to the jacket was a crumpled piece of paper with sequins pasted around it. The writing on the paper ended with these lines: "I shall not waste my days in trying to prolong them. I shall use my time." I wonder where that young man spent his last days or whether anyone washed his face and saw in it the hidden presence of the Divine, the sublime presence that labors to evolve in each of us? The radiance that cannot be entombed. The soul in matter that is the real Easter story.

Once on Easter dawn I drove to a small waterfall at the upper end of the city. The grass was soft around the falls, deep and moist. I turned at the sound of voices and realized that a large group of people were arriving. Evidently some church had planned an outdoor service at this very spot. Arms swinging, the makeshift congregation moved toward the falls carrying instruments and song sheets. No one seemed nonplussed by my presence. They greeted me as if I were the first to arrive. I laughed to myself. They must have advertised, and were delighted that a stranger responded.

When everyone gathered together the music began. There were prayers, readings… the familiar words of resurrection and victory. I still hadn't moved from my spot. They simply formed their worship around me. The sun was warm on my face. The desert sun. The sun of my forty days and forty nights. The sun of my untamed heart.

The sun of the human effort to touch God, of our searching through the dark, limited by dense, primitive ways. Still, we press on, our passages illumined by the very Light we are compelled to know. The one Soul whose vastness has created everything.

*We press on,
compelled to know,
to touch,
to love God.*

Love Demands Authenticity

 On the wall in the waiting room at the women's prison was a mural of Disney characters. Snow White. Cinderella. Sleeping Beauty. I wish the artist had painted different images, because prison life is not a fairy tale, and true love is not a "feel good" story.

Life and love require and demand authenticity. I wanted my message to the women to challenge them, not help them find a way to escape. Go beyond this immediate darkness and let a greater power speak, I intended to say. Ask it to reveal all the lies and small concessions with which you've betrayed yourself, the ways you've neglected your own heart and soul. Then start anew—this very day. Decide how to spend your hours. Decide whether or not to make the effort to grow. You can watch television, or have a real conversation. Healing is really a choice.

I knew it wasn't easy. Transforming familiar habits and patterns of thought requires courage. Forgiving and loving require deep intention. But we aren't alone. All creation awaits us.

I sat in front of Snow White and Cinderella and prayed for the women. Prayed for myself. Prayed for all of us to make courageous changes and choices. I prayed because I knew what would happen if we all let the Spirit within become our sight. I knew that prison wall or not, we'd be free.

Overcoming familiar habits and patterns takes courage.

Holding Things Lightly

My younger brother, Peter, was brain damaged when he was six months old. Spinal meningitis ravaged his body, taking everything but his breath.

Since we were close in age, I spent hours wheeling his carriage, or crawling up to sit beside him in the white screened enclosure my father had constructed so he could lie outside in the fresh breeze. A child, I was free from the questions that tormented my parents. Why did this happen? Could they have done more, sooner? Who would care for him when they could not?

I only felt the joy of him; the silent companionship. I knew delight when the wind blew across our cheeks and Peter laughed. It was a secret life, our own world. When he died at fifteen years of age, my heart was broken. Only in time would I grow to see his life, all our lives, as part of a much greater whole. I saw how each individual life is connected to a greater meaning, and that if I trusted that larger story, I would not be defeated by pain. My heart, in fact, began to break open into compassion, and I experienced a force of great love. This love asked me to relate to the things I treasured in a new way. To hold them lightly, regarding them as pure gift. As close as I was to my brother, it was only through the lens of this love that I began to see him for the first time.

Each life has meaning and is connected to a greater whole.

The Demands of Love

 Children reared in a country torn by war were asked to respond to the concept, love. "Love is nothing good," they wrote. "Love is suffering. Love is an illness and you have no medicine for it. Love is a feeling—you're possessed, like by a devil." It's tempting to believe I have a far greater understanding of love. I wonder. I may have better words to describe it, but I'm not certain that I see love any more clearly.

I used to think of love as something originating in me. I would say, "I love you," and imagine an emotion welling up in my heart. But in truth love originates from a reality that is not my own. The love that takes form in my character and nature is not "my" love. Love already exists.

This love asks for my willingness to go deeper. Will I confront my fear of knowing who I truly am? Love is the invisible hand that asks for my own hand and my own life, lived boldly. Love says, "This. This moment. Wait with me here this one hour."

It is not romantic. It is not sentimental. It is a burning fire within me. A great force. If I open to this love with all my heart, I will change.

Love originates from a reality that is not ours.

Giving Birth to a Deeper Love

 I am sitting in a circle of new friends in Eastern Europe. A man begins, "I was sent to Siberia when I was six and left when I was eighteen. My father lived there most of his life. We were forced to build roads, working all day for a single slice of bread." Tears fill his eyes. "Now we fight the communist legacy: anger and suspicion." Someone else speaks. "How is it possible that members of your family may barely respond to you, yet a stranger comes across thousands of miles and listens to our stories and there is a peculiar feeling between us? What is this feeling?"

I tell her it's called love. Past all our experiences, past man's inhumanity to man, past legacies of anger and fear, this small commodity: love.

The next morning I pass a church where a fiftieth wedding anniversary Mass will soon begin. The door is open and a young priest is placing tea lights alongside the thin carpet that reaches down the center aisle. There are no other adornments for the celebration.

From the doorway of the church I watch the anniversary couple and their family thread their way without ceremony through the village streets. The old woman carries a bouquet of garden flowers. Her husband holds her hand. Doors open as they pass and neighbors fall into step behind them.

I stay to watch, but the words spoken by the priest are in a foreign tongue. Still, watching these faces, and perhaps because I'm unencumbered by words, I realize I am watching the human story. I recognize the difficulty of walking toward love. I see why Peter faltered on the water. It is not circumstances that determine my path. It is whether or not I meet them with something greater.

Do we know how difficult it is to walk toward love?

Looking Through a Lens of Love

 Following my mother's death I drove back to her home, my childhood home. It was a little house on a hill in a small town, and nothing about it held any particular significance. The only meaning of those years was the meaning I brought to them. Each family member shared in the common events of that household, yet we all drew different interpretations and made up different stories. In later years I was struck by the way the individual perspectives we formed at that time had affected the choices we each made, and how these choices colored our lives. I wondered if we'd been capable of looking with the eyes of love, and not eyes clouded by expectation, or judgment, what we might have seen. How might our choices have been different?

So much is possible in our lives. We do not require a great stage, but only the willingness to live our ordinary lives with open hearts. In the play based on my life story, God turns to me and says, "Look at yourself, Paula. Really see yourself." When the actor playing the part of God delivers that line, I am always startled to attention. How am I relating to my life? Are my eyes open? My heart? Do I see what's right before me, or only what I'm programmed to see? What would it take to look with eyes of love?

We need only be willing to lead our lives with open hearts.

Being a Presence of Peace

We'd come together at the time of the new millennium in a wooded retreat center. Almost everyone had a different reason for being there—for choosing to usher in the new age with silence and reflection.

The days prior to New Year's Eve flowed easily. We shared in small groups, listened to music, and joined in rousing discussions, and each time we met there was a continuing discussion about how we would spend the midnight hour on December 31. We agreed that we would like to sing. But what? Could sixty-five persons reach a consensus? For two or three days we passed out hymnals and asked the participants to drop suggestions into a small basket. Majority would rule. I questioned how much agreement we would possibly find. Yet when the slips of paper were read, half of those attending had selected the same song: "Let There Be Peace on Earth."

It is a moment I will always hold dear. Not so much singing the words with all of us gathered together—though that was beautiful—but meaning the words in such a strong way. Owning them. Reckoning with the fact that if there is ever to be peace on earth, I will have to understand peace and live peace and be a presence of peace. Peace is not an idea. I'll either embody it, or not.

Peace is not an idea.
We must understand it and live it.

The Face of God

Everything begins with mystery, everything reflects mystery, everything is at the command of a Great Mystery. What will convince us? There's nothing to find. No mountain to climb. It only remains to walk along the road ahead, whatever that may be. Factory worker. Scholar. Father, son. Teacher. We have to align

*Only when we change
our inner selves
will the world change.*

DESIGN PICS

ourselves with the power already flowing through life. We have to stop opposing creation, and know this greater truth from within: Only when our inner universe changes (our thoughts, desires) will the outer world be affected.

I listened to an old teacher lecture a gymnasium filled with devotees. His words were lyrical, but I could write nothing down. I let his gentleness soothe me, caring more for his manner than his message. Then he paused, looking out at the hundreds who were gathered. "We're here so briefly," he whispered, almost inaudibly. "We're here so briefly."

If our eyes could only see that it is all the face of God. It was not only the apostles who walked and drank with him. Nothing is separate from the divine, nothing incidental. In thunderstorms, in our ordinary bowls of stew, in calloused hands that provide shelter and solace, in the drunk driver who kills your family. In all that is, one Spirit moves.

And if we could see, we would be overtaken by awe, and changed.

Paula D'Arcy's poignant reflections for this issue of *Daybreaks* will touch your heart in a way that can only move you closer to God. She explores the themes of love, fear, pain, and promise in ways that will move you emotionally, guide you spiritually, and make this Lent and Easter season a rewarding journey.

Begin your day with a *Daybreaks* meditation. Find a quiet, peaceful place. The reflections will only take a few moments, but allow time for the message to unfold in your heart. As it does, consider how these ideas impact your life, think about ways you can change your attitudes and beliefs, and hear the words, Come, follow me.

PAULA D'ARCY is an internationally known retreat leader and conference and seminar speaker. Her ministry grew out of tragedy. In 1975 her husband and twenty-one-month-old daughter were killed by a drunken driver. Paula survived the accident and gave birth to another daughter six months later. Paula is the author of several books, including these titles published by Crossroad Publishing Company: *When People Grieve: Overcoming Pain Through Love; Gift of the Red Bird: The Story of a Divine Encounter; Seeking with all My Heart: Encountering God's Presence in Scripture and Literature;* and *A New Set of Eyes: Encountering the Hidden God.* She is also the founder of the Red Bird Foundation, which ministers to people in prison, to the disadvantaged, and to those in need of healing.

© 2007, Liguori Publications, Liguori, MO 63057-9999
Imprimatur: Most Reverend Robert J. Hermann,
Auxiliary Bishop, Archdiocese of St. Louis
Printed in the USA. All rights reserved.
To order, call 1-800-325-9521. Visit us on the web at www.liguori.org.
Editor: Paul P. Pennick • Design: Pam Hummelsheim
Cover image: Design Pics

Liguori
ONE LIGUORI DRIVE
LIGUORI MO 63057-9999

ISBN 978-0-7648-1495-2

50000>

9

CICDRLE2